THE WESTERN BOOK OF THE DEAD

InterVarsity Press
P.O. Box 1400, Downers Grove, IL 60515-1426
World Wide Web: www.ivpress.com
E-mail: mail@ivpress.com

©1970 by InterVarsity Press

Revised edition ©2002 by InterVarsity Press

All rights reserved. No part of this book may be reproduced in any form without written permission from InterVarsity Press.

InterVarsity Press® is the book-publishing division of InterVarsity Christian Fellowship/USA®, a student movement active on campus at hundreds of universities, colleges and schools of nursing in the United States of America, and a member movement of the International Fellowship of Evangelical Students. For information about local and regional activities, write Public Relations Dept., InterVarsity Christian Fellowship/USA, 6400 Schroeder Rd., P.O. Box 7895, Madison, WI 53707-7895, or visit the IVCF website at <www.ivcf.org>.

ISBN 0-87784-136-5

Printed in the United States of America ∞

P 13 12 11 10 9 8 7 6 5 4 3 2 1

Y 11 10 09 08 07 06 05 04 03 02

Preface

The following document was unearthed in a recent archaeological dig. Its fragments paint a picture of a civilization from its rise to its decline. This once-great empire is now lost to the ages, but its chronicle here listed, with its myths of origins and self-understanding, offers us valuable lessons, if only we will listen.

The language of this ancient people is curious but not altogether indecipherable. The editors have attempted to render it accessible to a contemporary audience without sacrificing the voice of antiquity. The author is unknown.

The translation committee

A.D. 2002

I

In the beginning
(that is, before the beginning)
there was
    NOTHING.
And MATTER came out of NOTHING.
    And MATTER was CHAOS.

II

Strangely, and for no reason whatsoever,
    CHAOS started to change.
Simplicity begat complexity,
    randomness begat order and,
most peculiar of all,
        inanimate MATTER begat
        organic MATTER.

III

Many, many, many years passed.

And quite by chance, organic MATTER
    developed in a strange direction.
It became more complex, and then
    for no apparent reason at all,
    it became conscious of itself.
It called consciousness MIND,
    and it gave itself a name.
And that name was HUMANITY.

IV

Now HUMANITY equipped with MIND
found that MIND played peculiar
tricks on MEN AND WOMEN.
Instead of just accepting HUMANITY as
part of MATTER, they began to
desire significance; they longed
to live for a purpose.

Instead of being pushed about by blind
chance, they wanted instead to
direct their own affairs.
They also found a state of being that was
entirely satisfactory to them.
And they called it LOVE.

V

HUMANITY kept searching for purpose
and meaning, and after a while
strange rumors began to spread—
    rumors that spoke of a creator who
    was LOVE, who had created
    HUMANITY in his own image.
Many believed the rumors.
They saw their lives taking on meaning
    and their universe being not so
    purposeless after all.

Inspired by hope, these BELIEVERS started
> to write,
> to paint and
> to chip away at blocks of stone.

Some were extremely skillful, seeming to express the longings and aspirations of all
> HUMANITY.

To their exceptional pieces of craft, a name was given, and that name was ART. And those who
> wrote them,
> painted them or
> chipped them out

were called ARTISTS.
And all their ART said:
> HUMANITY IS SIGNIFICANT.

VI

It was also rumored that the
   creator LOVE had a son.
This SON OF LOVE became a man,
   showed HUMANITY how to live,
      and then died.
Legend has it that the SON OF LOVE
   soon came back from the dead
   and disappeared in a cloud.
This legend led some BELIEVERS to spread
the message further that
   HUMANITY IS SIGNIFICANT.

VII

For many years this state of affairs existed.

LOVE and SIGNIFICANCE
    were joined together.
But HUMANITY became restless.
    Was it so?
    Was HUMANITY a creation of
              LOVE?
    Why believe a rumor?
    Had anyone used REASON (a very
    special activity of MIND that had

proved to be successful in understanding MATTER) to find out if the rumor was true?
Did the rumor actually correspond to what really was?

A thorough investigation began in the WEST, and it lasted many years.

VIII

After an era of investigation, the WEST came to certain conclusions:

1. The rumors were certainly false. REASON found no EVIDENCE to verify the creation hypothesis. A creator was the result of wishful daydreams, a figment of IMAGINATION—which itself was an early aberration in primitive HUMANITY, now happily under the

control of REASON.
And if the rumor of a creator was false, so surely was the complex rumor about his son.

2. HUMANITY was not significant—some mysterious higher being. On the contrary, HUMANITY was of no importance at all—simply a complex product of cause and effect, a meaningless piece of MATTER on a larger but equally meaningless piece of MATTER called earth.

HUMANITY had emerged from a primordial slime and was really neither more nor less than that.

IX

At first nothing much changed.
But a few years passed, and a perceptive
few began to notice a difference.
> Music didn't seem to sound
> > the same.
> Paintings didn't look
> > the same.
> Books didn't read in
> > the same way.

Some started to complain, but the ARTISTS
(always very honest, transparent people)
simply said:

"We are interpreting REALITY. If
>   REALITY is meaningless, then we
>   must imitate that meaninglessness.
> You must not give yourselves airs.
>   You are NOTHING.
> You are a conscious bit of protoplasm
>   condemned to death on this planet."

At that, the critics stopped carping and
started saying how beautiful the
NEW ART was.

They didn't want to use the word *beautiful*—
everybody knew it didn't mean anything—
but it had been around for so long that they
decided,

why not?

X

Then too a few noticed changes in the way MEN AND WOMEN behaved.
> Along the way they had found that they loved each other. And this love was thought to be a reflection of the LOVE who had created them.

But LOVE was not MATTER.
And only MATTER was significant.
So gradually
> LOVE became irrelevant.

Now there was just SEX—
  liaisons of the moment.
And families began to die, and the fates
  of children were left to the whim of
    courts. And they called these
      liaisons
        LOVE.

They knew, however, that the word *love*
  didn't mean anything.

XI

All sorts of startling consequences followed.
Some said,
> "If HUMANITY is only a machine
> caught up in the vast mechanism of
> nature, why not act accordingly?"

So MANIPULATORS set to work and
used HUMANITY just like other
objects of nature.

And there came a very efficient system called
UTOPIA, and the occupants were
given numbers in place of names.

(Of course, it was really nothing new, for
the MANIPULATORS had picked
up their model from the ANTS, a
natural group of beings who years
previously had attained the perfect
state of affairs.)
Another group resisted UTOPIA. They said,
"In spite of all that REASON has proved,
we will continue to believe that our
longings and aspirations are meaningful."
So they tried to forget their DESPAIR
(a feeling that HUMANITY
experienced when wanting to hope
and hoping while knowing that all
was hopeless).
They worshiped nonsense

in place of sense,
and they called it
the ABSURD.
But soon this bored them, and they
began to worship EXPERIENCE.
They took chemicals and behaved
like animals, living only for each
successive moment and trying hard
to make each moment pleasurable.
Most of them got tired after a while and
disposed of themselves in various ways.
Some went to DEATH,
some to ECSTASY (a beautiful
country with a synthetic landscape)
and some to NIRVANA.
Some even returned to UTOPIA.

Elsewhere REASON was abandoned—
because, you see, it couldn't give
answers to the really big questions
after all. In its place came unreason,
and they called it RELATIVISM.
Likewise, MORALITY was abandoned—
because that peculiar ability to
distinguish between THE GOOD
and THE BAD was regarded as a
mere matter of taste or caprice.
THE GOOD and THE BAD had been
popular once, but that was when
rumors of the creator LOVE
were rife.
(THE GOOD was the creator's character
and had to be obeyed.

THE BAD was disobedience or revolt
   against THE GOOD.)
But THE GOOD and THE BAD departed
   with REASON and LOVE.
   And now there was
      no longer tragedy—
         only MISERY.

XII

So HUMANITY ceased to be human—
a rational, moral creation which once
 transcended the causality of nature.
Instead there stood a meaningless,
 enigmatic machinelike piece of
  MATTER.
Even the MANIPULATORS who

controlled UTOPIA ceased to be
human in the old sense of the word.
After denying their HUMANITY for so
long, they finally lost it and so
became the most terrifying animal
on the face of the earth.

Postscript

The old rumors still persist,
>   found in outlying regions and small
>   cliques of NONCONFORMISTS
>   in UTOPIA:

>   LOVE IS.

Some even say that HUMANITY still is.

But these are the same ones who say
that no one has ever really died,
> that even the ancients are alive
> (some well, some not)
> and living in an

OTHER WORLD.

Such rumors are being suppressed
> wherever they are found.

Editor's Afterword

The Western Book of the Dead sheds light on a civilization we are only gradually coming to understand. Scholars of this civilization are rapidly disseminating their findings on a variety of topics surrounding this groundbreaking fragment. Some such works are classified below.

REASON
Escape from Reason by Francis Schaeffer
Give Me a Reason by Cliffe Knechfle
Know Why You Believe by Paul Little
Reason in the Balance by Phillip E. Johnson
Truth Decay by Douglas Groothuis
Why Should Anyone Believe Anything at All? by
    James W. Sire

LOVE
Eros Defiled by John White
Tainted Love by David Mark Brown
True Love in a World of False Hope by
    Robbie Castleman

CREATOR
Darwin on Trial by Phillip E. Johnson
How Blind Is the Watchmaker? by Neil Broom
Intelligent Design by William Dembski

SON OF LOVE
The Challenge of Jesus by N. T. Wright
Jesus with Dirty Feet by Don Everts

HUMANITY
Being Human by Ranald Macaulay & Jerram Barrs
The Universe Next Door by James W. Sire

IMAGINATION
Art & Soul by Hilary Brand & Adrienne Chaplin
The Creative Life by Alice Bass
Imagine by Steve Turner
Scribbling in the Sand by Michael Card

More research is being done every day. Visit

<www.ivpress.com>

for more information on the civilization described in this document and its implications for our own.